Patterns
in Nature

Bela Davis

Abdo Kids Junior
is an Imprint of Abdo Kids
abdopublishing.com

Abdo
PATTERNS ARE FUN!
Kids

abdopublishing.com

Published by Abdo Kids, a division of ABDO, P.O. Box 398166, Minneapolis, Minnesota 55439.

Printed in the United States of America, North Mankato, Minnesota.

052018

092018

THIS BOOK CONTAINS
RECYCLED MATERIALS

Photo Credits: iStock, Shutterstock

Production Contributors: Teddy Borth, Jennie Forsberg, Grace Hansen

Design Contributors: Christina Doffing, Candice Keimig, Dorothy Toth

Library of Congress Control Number: 2017960616

Publisher's Cataloging-in-Publication Data

Names: Davis, Bela, author.

Title: Patterns in nature / by Bela Davis.

Description: Minneapolis, Minnesota : Abdo Kids, 2019. | Series: Patterns are fun! |
    Includes glossary, index and online resources (page 24).

Identifiers: ISBN 9781532107962 (lib.bdg.) | ISBN 9781532108945 (ebook) |
    ISBN 9781532109430 (Read-to-me ebook)

Subjects: LCSH: Pattern perception--Juvenile literature. | Nature--Juvenile literature. |
    Mathematics--Miscellanea--Juvenile literature.

Classification: DDC 006.4--dc23

Table of Contents

Patterns in Nature

Patterns can be seen all over.

Even in nature!

A pattern is an order that is repeated. A lot of things can make one.

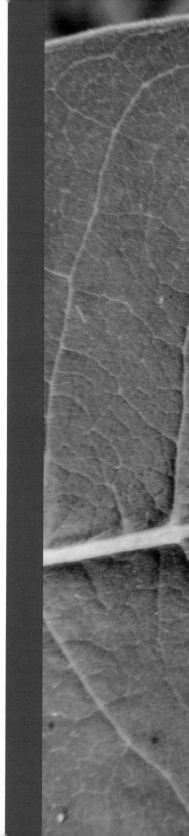

Look inside fruit! The shapes can make a pattern. The colors can too.

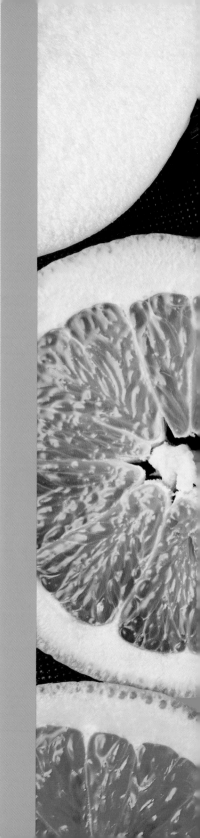

Buzz! Bees have stripes.

It is a pattern.

Shells can have a pattern.

Snails have **spiral** shells.

Trees have rings. Count them.

How old is the tree?

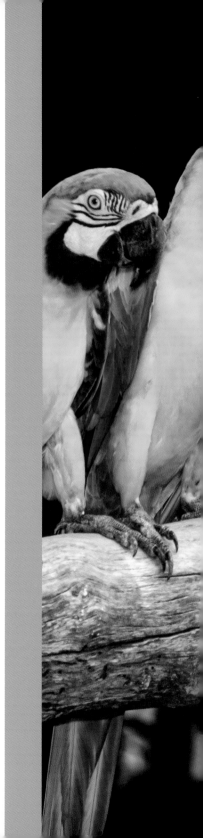

Macaws sit on a log. They make a pattern.

Tulips are pretty! The colors make a pattern.

19

Look around. Do you see
a pattern?

Some Types of Patterns

color pattern

object pattern

shape pattern

symmetry pattern

Glossary

macaw
any of a number of brightly colored, tropical American parrots with long, slightly curved tails.

spiral
a curve that circles around and gets bigger or smaller as it moves away from a fixed point.

Index

Abdo Kids ONLINE
FREE! ONLINE MULTIMEDIA RESOURCES

Visit **abdokids.com** and use this code to access crafts, games, videos, and more!

Abdo Kids Code:
PPK7962